The Smooth White Vanishing

Poems

copyright 2005

Also by Toni Thomas:

Chosen	Brick Road Poetry Press
Fast as Lightening	Gribble Press
Walking on Water	Finishing Line Press
Blue Halo	Annalese Press
Ace Raider of the Unfathomable Universe	Annalese Press
You'll be Fast as Lightning Coveting my Painted Tail	Annalese Press
Hotsy Totsy Ballroom	Annalese Press
Love Adrift in the City of Stars	Annalese Press
In the Pink Arms of the City	Annalese Press
In the Kingdom of Longing	Annalese Press
The Things We Don't Know	Annalese Press
In the Boarding House for Unclaimed Girls	Annalese Press
They Became Wing Perfect and Flew	Annalese Press
Unburdened Kisses	Annalese Press
Bandits Come and Remove Her Body in the Night	Annalese Press
There is This	Annalese Press
Here	Annalese Press

The Smooth White Vanishing

Poems

First published in 2023 by Annalese Press
134 Towngate
Netherthong
Holmfirth
West Yorkshire HD9 3XZ
England

Copyright © 2004 Toni Thomas

Please Note
All characters and situations appearing
in these pages are in the service of poetry.
Any resemblance to real persons,
living or dead, is purely coincidental.

All rights reserved. No part of this publication may be reproduced, stored, or transmitted in any form, or by any means electronic, mechanical or photocopying, recording or otherwise, without the express written permission of the publisher.

Cover design and layout by Peter Wadsworth
Painting – *Symphony in White, #1: The White Girl*
James McNeill Whistler, 1862, National Gallery of Art

British Library Cataloguing-in-Publication Data
A catalogue record for this book is available on request from the British Library.

ISBN 978-1-7394457-2-0

Acknowledgments

"The Smooth White Vanishing" appeared in *Lullwater Review*

"Magic Act" appeared in *Eclipse*

"An Education" appeared in *HazMat Review*

Contents

Part One *White*

Invisible	3
White	5
An Education	6
Mother	7
The Smooth White Vanishing	8
The Hair Cut	11
Wakefield Pond	13
Thanks Giving	15
I Wanted to Believe	16
Glass Eyes	17
Autumn is Lax with Bald Trees	19

Part Two *Snatched*

Homecoming Queen	23
Downstream Recovery Project	26
At the Produce Stand off I-84 in Gresham	28
Marion	29
Terrible Things Can Happen	30
Snatched	32
Disappears	33
The Apricot Lover	35
Big Pumpkins in Small Wheelbarrows	37

Part Three *The Color of Emptiness*

A Coward, I Run Away ...	43
It Was Such a Season	44
Purgatory	45
Prayer	46
Shoeless	47
Riddled with Bees	48

The Man Who Imagined Me X-Rated ...	49
After the Timbre of Your Lovely Hands ...	50
The Color of Emptiness	51
Magic Act	52
Snow	54

Last night as I was sleeping,
I dreamt—marvelous error!—
that a spring was breaking
out in my heart.
I said: Along which secret aqueduct,
oh water, are you coming to me,
water of a new life
that I have never drunk?

Last night as I was sleeping,
I dreamt—marvelous error!—
that I had a beehive
here inside my heart.
And the golden bees
were making white combs
and sweet honey
from my old failures.

Antonio Machado

PART ONE
White

Invisible

The woman two seats down
in the brown armchair
has made herself small
stares out the cafe window
as if the world's adjectives have fled
collapsed inside the arms
of September's mauling.

But then shrunkenness happens—
my uncle who lost his job welding steel
now welds beer bottles to his hand
my mama's black painted walls
marking her hand's derision
me - red faced hydrant
some diseased day dragged in
not picture perfect as
the girls in my 8th grade class
with their straight teeth
hairless legs leaning on weight machines
numerical versions of happiness
that handrail the day.

Cut me some slack my dad tells me
says I have a glass eye to see the world
time bomb ready to detonate.
He likes to complain about things
no giblets in the gravy
Friday's fish dinner without the tartar sauce
my mother's pale excuse for a salad.

I have grown weary as tarnished silver
factory workers
timecards with no mercy

neighbors who chain smoke
shuffle around in terry house slippers
avoid the vague remembrance of paradise
that once chimed in their beds.

This place will never be powder puff perfect
my dad tells me, *get used to it*
get used to the crusted ice
pinned butterfly wings
the fact that some things
come to nothing in this world.
He shrugs his shoulders
takes another gulp of his Pepsi
refuses to plague his brain with
the yard's maligned thistle.

I grind lemon into my bathwater
attrition, my brother's lost voice
father's sobriety
the way my mother caves into her day
devours bowl after bowl of late night ice cream
when something incomprehensible
weeps beneath the floor.

White

Here today, gone tomorrow
that's what my mother used to say
as consolation
as if I'm supposed to take
the big piece of the pie
not wait till tomorrow
when nothing might be left
death happens, she knew that
didn't want me to postpone
my entry at the gate.

I ran after that
ran through schoolyards
college classrooms, bags of candy
days with too much bust
ran through men
so they'd never contain me
not as in some neat life
with a foursquare house
two kids, lawn mower
chain link fence towing.

We never talked about the disappearing
I reserved that for cake batter
white as virgin sin
cargo trunks, window seats
as if the future
would have to look back at me
so slender
never derailed in the rain.

Oh yes, how in vanishing myself
I did shine.

An Education

My father never retires the
newspaper from his hands
recites car wrecks, oil spills, obituaries
broken marriages
the forecast of rain
in a sun soaked world.

I wake up one day
a memorization table
white sheets on a taut clothesline
thank god for parasites
crooked hems.

The people in my world
grow concrete feet
barely talk to me anymore
my mother forgets how to dance
lacquers her hair
to keep the wind from blistering.

I stand up on tiptoe
want to see past the fence
grow stick thin on cake batter
the white surety
uncomplicated way
it slides down my throat
makes me tapered as my father's love
as the miles of newspaper column
he rattles away.

Mother

convinced you can fly
you mount the sky
set aside your asters, big wig
fishnet stockings
housewife perfect.
Nobody wants meatloaf at this curb.

It is blinking crazy somebody tells me.
I am 14, a crème puff
have never heard of mothers going AWOL
but you have a penchant for ocean
hennaed hair
beach parties, clam digging
are tired of shoveling snow
ambushing the neighbor
to jump start our car.

I learn to handle a can opener
heat t.v. dinners, ravioli.
After three months my baby brother
says he doesn't even miss you anymore
my dad blames the man next door
all those surefire claims of paradise
he's lodged in your head.

Weekends my brother and I
lay awake under the bed sheets
count cars, birds, clouds
wait on your dented Chevy to pull up
travel your shapely legged body
blue chorus back to us.

The Smooth White Vanishing

Ultimately god saves
that's what my mother says
after my first marriage fails
after cake batter starts miring
the long length of my hair.
She says the same thing eighteen summers
earlier when my dad puts his fist
through the screen door
and she is elsewhere
in those fishnet stockings
that always divided them.

The summer of '79 was a scorching heat wave
window fans sold out in the store
my dad's tomato plants wilting
as fast as the leaf lettuce.
It's the year he lost his job after complaining
about unfair promotion practices
and my mom said he never knew how to play ball
was as unlikely as a fish in kerosene
to make a big splash.
I stayed in my room
my mother brought her cargo trunk
out from the basement
said she needed a break from the heat
from our cramped Queens apartment
headed to Plymouth
where her mother and father once owned that
big porched farmhouse on Cherry Street
and all her summers were spent life guarding

riding horses, playing tag with big muscled men
whose promise stayed glued to their bodies
like bronzed skin.

On September 2nd she came back through the door
said *school is starting, the kids need new clothes*
poured a bag of chipped beach shells
onto the kitchen table, fired up the kettle.
My brother and I cried all morning
glad for small miracles, our fears elbowed out
of living with a bitter man the rest of our days.

But my father, he was different
resolute as his orphanage days
stayed more than arm's length away
complained about the lumpy gravy
overcooked meat
mashed potatoes that taste fake.
We bought more fudge marble ice cream
my dad sent out over one hundred job applications
but never landed one
just turned forty, taught himself how to drive
got his license
never found another full time job
secretly confirmed to himself
that like his dead mother
years in the orphanage
nobody in the end will be there
started doing accounting for tax season
three months out of the year

stayed sulky behind the newspaper headlines
circled job ads, wrote letters to the editor.

After a while my mother's fishnet stockings didn't fit
when I was sixteen she wanted to teach me to samba
couldn't remember the moves
at nineteen I ran off to England on school loans
a college exchange program
waited ten years to come back
first saw that handsome bearded Englishman
on the slopes of Austria (the one I'd later marry)
made a vow to become long
tapered as a vanilla bean
ice cream smooth, white
as I rolled down his throat.

The Hair Cut

When my mother chopped my bangs
so short I thought the whole world
wore ugly sweaters
it was no use telling her
she never saw the sense in paying money
for a straight cut
you'll look great she'd say
wielding the scissor
scuffing her socks around in my fallen hair.

When my mother chopped my bangs
tried to curl the ends of my long hair with a hot roller
and my father spent another sleepless night
tossing empty words out the back door
I decided heaven has green fangs
and only girls with at least fifty lashes
ever get to eat there.

It was the summer of my 16th birthday
my mother was letting go of herself
and her once dreams of the sea.
I wrote my name in the layers of dust
blanketing her cargo trunks
swore I would never let the things I love
be reduced to graffiti
never marry a man who holds anger
fierce as a caged dog
girds his teeth against a world
turned greedy.

My new husband has fierce treatises
under soft words
doesn't want to move where I am heading

learned his rhetoric from the debate team
at some elite boarding school.
The flowers in my garden grow crippled
in harsh light, wilt under petulant hands.

We have two little children
a whittling away of recklessness in our lives
airtight as rabbit hutches.
My husband the once fiction writer
with his address book of attorneys
in case I try to move back east.
He tells me *you'll never get to take the kids*.
These are the terms we live by
they are noxious, make for no good sex
a field of promise turned rancid.

My mother chopped my bangs impulsively
her good intentions as firm
as her pummeled heart
my husband chops invisibly
one clip at a time
whittles away kisses
my deepest loves
till I am a box of matchsticks.

Wakefield Pond

My parents went there on weekends
to the two bedroom cabin
that nested in thick pine above water.
In high school I saved my retail money
bought them a small sailboat
with a removable keel
enough to get them out to the center
of the pond without drowning.

My father never did learn how to tack
back and forth across the water
adjust the sail, let the wind guide him.
They went out twice, my father confused
then angry at the impudent ropes
my mother, the former life guard
squirming as she crouched low
so the loose boom wouldn't smack her.

It probably makes a difference that my father
was raised in a Bronx orphanage
never shown by the nuns how to ride a bicycle
change a faucet washer, reignite a stove.
Forty years old before he learned how to drive a car.

Afterwards, my mother only ever went out
on the wide swath of the pond
circled the islands
with one of the succession of boyfriends
I brought home over the years
to her they were educated, capable men
she was convinced wouldn't drown her.

The cabin at Wakefield Pond was perched
above clear water near the Ossipee Mountains.

My parents came there to forget the city
forget their past
worked hard to keep the fallen leaves
blackberry vines from overtaking.

Sometimes love is a thin wafer
grows perilous
the pond gets missed in moonlight
a sliver between tall pines
sometimes there is a boat
capsizable, small as a donut hole
you stake your life on, enter
life jackets the color of orange fish
the islands not too far away
the crescent of cabins on the other side beckoning
the speedboats already gone home to decay

soon you are skimming the water
learning to duck your head
swing the sail back and forth on its
cheap coil of rope
not minding the cheapness
it's the gliding
the gliding you were after
some blind faith that has
held you to trust
the buoyancy of water
again and again.

Thanks Giving

We make clothes pins into stick children
pilgrims with printed dresses, paper hats
erect a barn, wooly sheep.

My father wears pain like a crusted shirt
dinner jacket he can barely fit in.
Nobody crosses his path without
their words clipped.

I dig hope out of my pocket
place it on the table
like a decent flashlight
turkeys in the side yard
next to the axe handle
impervious to the squeeze of fate.

Tomorrow we will thank God abruptly
then eat
cranberry, bird, gravy, stuffing, potatoes
the sheer abundance, way the plenty
the scraping of the plates
erases what we can't be.

How deftly we navigate absence
the creator of good things
forgives our trespasses
rewards even the least of us

for in the kingdom of want
we are perfectly blessed.

I Wanted to Believe

that in his great white heroic crazed lust for my mother
all vices would be crowbarred away
not flap soiled cotton on a sun fevered clothesline.

For seventeen years we wore our implacable grins
waited on chipped knees
for the house to dismount, find its foundation.

Is it incorrigible to eat up the cold
let it live in you
like a penance for something you may
or may not have done
the world's quotient of happiness flapping?

In December my mother stops
setting the kettle to brew
erases the moon from her face
stomps on the linoleum floor, dies there
too young to die
too exhausted to grow old here.
The smashed blue willow tea cup
body laid out, incinerated
tossed out across two coasts.

A year later my father remarries
five years later ships me my mother's wedding ring
the one from Bavaria when he was an army lieutenant
18 karat gold with a pair of holes
where two of a cluster of diamonds went missing.
Elaborate ring. The fret, weight of it.
Hastily I bury it in the closet
imagine even amidst the vanishing
how it once must have shined.

Glass Eyes

When worship was a small word
I held on my lips
and the night a measure of betrayal
my brother and I swept aside
my father's incendiary eye
built a fort.
I wanted to be anonymous
not claimed by the cruelty of his love
the way he burnt paper, beetles
bad children in the heat of his gaze.

Christmas came and went without
the room burning
but the lookout couldn't always be trusted
my father's eye a vacuum that sucks up
dolls, ribbon, paint pots, marbles
leaves metal machinery.
I tell my brother to be vigilant
but he doesn't listen
becomes the roller coaster with too many dips.

Through hell and high water
I keep my fort bolstered
hive in creamy substances
their unserpentine mien
angel food cake, ice cream
cookies with a soft layer—
imagine them being eaten invisible
one by one till they become me.

Over time
my father grows old
gets glass eyes

makes believe he can see
but he can't.
I stroke caterpillars
resurrect the boy
fallen through the pond ice
bring back to life yard beetles.

There isn't anything I can't do now
with the absences he has laid.

Autumn is Lax with Bald Trees

green tomatoes the sun refuses to turn red.
I rake leaves, the anatomy of fear
remember afternoons of kick ball
my brother's body buried in leaves
the tenderness of fingers that
rupture the skin's tight face.

In the field, vines of crooked shaped
pumpkins are ripening.
We will carve toothy grins
prop them on the front stoop
let their candles burn under
the moon's white gauze.

I remember my past
the fruit I set there
hope I wore like a bright pendant
dangling gold into the night air
the conference of blue gloves
disappeared lady slippers
my mother with her warm breath
calling my brother and I home
to anoint the soup she had made.

PART TWO
Snatched

Homecoming Queen

When my Aunt Joan's daughter DeeDee
was chosen to be city Homecoming Queen
my whole family gave a dinner to celebrate
after all, she was the youngest
the runt of the litter Uncle used to say
because her childhood was muddied with
croup, asthma inhalers, allergies
and a bout of pneumonia.
My Aunt Joan claimed that unlike the other three kids
she put on twenty pounds and it stayed
DeeDee *the creme puff* because of her
porcelain skin, snow white hair
DeeDee *the shrimp*, DeeDee *the fallen princess*
after another scrape slipping off the porch stairs
DeeDee *the flower girl with glass wings*.
We were all expected to treat her with kid gloves
no dust mites, dog or cat hair
no rough housing, wearing her out with tag.

At eighteen she'd blossomed into a size seven beauty.
The class yearbook voted her *most likely to succeed*
reeled off ten clubs plus baton twirling below her name.
She had a boyfriend, Rex, from the football team
who was twelve inches taller
and we had no idea what she'd do with all that popularity
once her reign as Homecoming Queen was over.

My mom and aunt spent hours flitting through magazines
trying to come up with just the right dress
till Aunt Joan stomped her feet
said if they couldn't find anything decent
they'd just have to make it themselves.

I cringed at the thought -
my mother the slumped hem sewer and Aunt Joan
sentimental as sin dressmaking some poufy gown
with sloped shoulders, too many layers
of unevenly stitched lace.

Fortunately, DeeDee was a sharp girl
and steered them clear away toward
the Miss Cascadia Dress Shop
on 59th and Hubert in Salem City.
My mom dragged me there, probably
so I could watch DeeDee slip effortlessly
into all those size 7 chiffon gowns, reform my ways
take my place among the legends of coquettish
young women who were sure to find
a charming man, vexless life.
It was sickening to watch all the fawning that afternoon
DeeDee in pink rayon off the shoulder with a long trail
DeeDee in vanilla bean brocade with pearl buttons
corseting the bodice
DeeDee in petal soft yellow floating in layers of chiffon
with matching satin heels.
Finally they settled on the peach taffeta
with the dropped waist plus a shawl
that looked like a boa constrictor
and slim crown of fake diamonds
to flame in her hair.

In June 2001 DeeDee became Homecoming Queen.
I must admit her skin was flawless, her entrance giddy
as someone who has all her schoolgirl dreams come true.
We took lots of pictures.

Later, uncle bought her a 1995 red Toyota
for doing such a dedicated job over her reign.
The next year I never went to my prom.
Imagined I did, showed up with no date
wearing a black rayon off the shoulder dress
with a single camellia and tennis shoes.

After her term as Homecoming Queen
DeeDee did not enjoy a vexless life, loyal husband
ended up divorced at 32 with three kids
a house and a pool mortgaged up to the eyeballs.
Everybody said it was Rex's fault, that he never grew up
after the high school football days
couldn't stomach a 9 to 6 work schedule
sitting at some computer terminal
walked out with a younger blonde.

DeeDee works an office job in Oregon City.
My uncle hired an attorney to track Rex down
somewhere in Chicago, press him for alimony.

DeeDee's asthma is acting up worse lately
she needs to keep her inhaler with her at all times
along with the meds.
My Aunt Joan watches the three kids.

DeeDee *the flower girl with glass wings*.
I always felt she was destined
for a finer life than this one.

Downstream Recovery Project

It was just before New Year
Aunt Dolores left her house
never came back.
They say Alzheimers will do that
steal the pictures from any family's wall
make the world diffuse
almost forgettable
as you muddle your way through traffic
enter the dark sixty five miles of woods
off Jaffrey Road
find peculiar angels slumped in trees
ponytailed monks, babies.

My mother says the police combed
the woods for three weeks
before calling off the search.
It was January, the heavy snows.
Uncle Trask went back in spring
says he found her virgin mary neck piece
about fifty yards from the river
says for sure she probably drowned
her body a downstream recovery project
they'll find someday.

Does the river gather up what the
world forgets
did she slip from her life, rose stippled walls
into another kind of robust scenery
place jewel beaded

made more of softly powdered earth
then chronic disdain?

One day will my own breath
float away
will I enter the river spread wide
like a fan, accordion drenched
rain smacked, muted
armed with a searchlight
looking for god again?

At the Produce Stand off I-84 in Gresham

She knows something must be here
dependable as clover, the cat with three lives
that the weight of a certain hand carries us
past the thrum of alarm clock
hasty toast, bagged lunches, neon

that she will live amid honeysuckle someday
get a trailer, plunk it down by the coast
in a park with hookups, decent bird watching
will live in the space between paragraphs
hobble a home
make lust into a daily tribunal
where beauty embraces crooked teeth
the body's knobby curves
makes a feast plate
out of the earth's uninsured scenery
the forests, coastline
tomatoes, dill, chard
that color our plate.

She greets strangers, children
weighs green beans, cabbage
bundles cilantro
counts coin
floats roma apples into their bags.

Marion

You used to come here as a boy
on the way to Ossipee
when Frank's I.G.A. was still open
and Marion lived up the hill
away from the clutch of cars
carefully prescribed lives
lived in the clapboard farmhouse gone faded.

It was a long time ago
her plum stained dress
old three-speed
the chanterelles, field daisies in
cans strapped onto her frame.

She died a few years back
alone with her cats, black lab
in the white house with green shutters.
There are photographs of them
somewhere back in that other life
a man's longing can barely reach.

You used to come here as a boy
a young man really
when your parents were still together
mapping all their plans.
She never fit into those
no college ambition, eagerness to make
some business contract with the world
her porch studded with honeysuckle
off key songs
hands that ambitioned your body
without ever raking.

Terrible Things Can Happen

Pregnant wife
with a drunken sailor
who goes east
loses his way home
the guillotined past
Asian paper doll trailing.

When the boy comes
she raises him alone
in a two room flat in Queens.
He will know absence
a crowded daycare, swollen feet
by age six how to cook noodles
bandage her knee, brew coffee
be the friend she's never had
keep the wolf gated

at sixteen gets a job after school
restocking shelves
quits when her chest starts cramping.
Evenings they play checkers, dominoes
conspire against the rain.

She fears one day he'll grow up, fly away.
He tells her what she wants to hear
that he will never desert her
they'll save money, move to the Jersey shore
eat steak sandwiches
float the water

their boat will finally come in
with its sturdy sail.

She smiles, knows he doesn't mean it
that terrible things can happen in this world
knows she has kept the key to his heart locked tight
one day there will be a rumble
another man who loses his way home
an irrevocable vanishing

Snatched

Melissa had never heard of a cricket
with three tongues
Jamie tells her -
it has three tongues and
a loathesome breath.

Today the sky black as coal
her cat poster, wall lamp, blue fairy gone
sucked into the creature's mouth.
Covetous cricket.
Bring it back Melissa shouts
*I want my room glued back beside
the left wall of the stairwell.*

Because Melissa is a gullible girl
with a wild streak of scarlet in her head
the cricket relents
spits her room back
at the spot she has groomed
with red galoshes, a stuffed leopard
irksome bear.

There now Melissa sighs
and the world feels right.
She pulls on her fleece night dress
presses her face to the window
where Mrs. Delaney's army of pumpkins
are growing fat as soccer balls down below
those dependable ringside miracles
that a room with the right view lends.

Disappears

Karl didn't want to hear
she was going away again.
She'd gone away before—in April
then back in February and in October for five days
using some excuse about *fall leaves turning color*
to make her escape.
He was beginning to feel like he was disposable
as in snot rag, rusted radiator
husband with no backbone
to insist what he needs.

She kept saying *you do want me to grow don't you*
how could she live a mundane life
without suffocating.
It did make sense on some level
he never liked the tedium either
the school schedule, piano lessons
dance, soccer, lawn mowing, yard work
car headaches, her irritability over meals
the kids' piled up laundry.

Maybe, Karl thought, he needed that too
the vanishing
to say he was leaving for the day, the weekend
the month, and not let anybody know where.
Just gone. They'd have to function without him
like he had to function without her.
Father disappears from his computer terminal
seen flying over the Golden Gate Bridge
with only his boxer shorts, a transistor radio.

What would people think of him then?
Of course she'd say he was selfish

putting himself first, dumping
the kids' lives in her lap.
Others would say he was a loser
irresponsible, must have snapped
his brain to let go of everything
walk away.

Some might say he was courageous
to sacrifice so much
in the name of the unknown
to be the hero of his own vanishing
but the last group were few
and far apart and generally well versed
in the templates of despair
broken vows, bankruptcies
to know a blank slate
when they see one
would tell him there are many
ways to vanish
many shapes, sizes, contours
when you cut yourself loose
and fall.

The Apricot Lover

He'd never heard the name before
Gunther, Helen Gunther
lived here eighty years ago
died alone in the back corner bedroom
laid there for three days and nights
before the delivery boy noticed the porch
backed up with soured milk bottles
called the police.
The wallpaper in the study showing its age
foxes and hunters, partridges
peonies gracing the corner bedroom
but faded, almost beige where
the sun bled through.
At one time there was a porch
and two wicker armchairs according to the
black and white photos down at the
Historical Society on Main.

Miss Helen Gunther, unmarried
aunt to Herbert, Savory, Emma, and Natalie Gunther
by way of her oldest brother, Walter
aunt to Daniel, Rice, Tabatha, and Amory Sills
by way of her middle sister's marriage
survived by Miss Ingrid Gunther
youngest, devoted sister who lived with Helen
looked after her for twenty odd years
till Mr. Harry Franklin came to town
opened the new podiatrist's shop
wooed her into a late engagement
being mother to his almost grown kids.

Helen the wallflower, apricot lover.
Helen of the fine silk purses, tiny feet.
Everyone said she was almost invisible

the way she lived
snipped off the dead heads of roses
watched for hours as the brown headed thrush
nibbled her seed
hummingbirds sipped at the ruby orb of her feeder.

In the final years her hair was still long
down to her waist but totally silver
tied up in a loose bun, anchored with turquoise
her arthritic hands still able to hold slim volumes of verse
shuck beans, brace the tomatoes
loop her lilies onto stout poles
beckon the moon to her bed
breath in that other
more invisible
kind of ether.

Big Pumpkins in Small Wheelbarrows

Venetian blind down
that's the way she keeps her parlor
come summer when the sun is
too much to allow in more than a mite.
Quaint some people call her
as if she is out of fashion really
a season of dwarf roses
slumped porch rafters, jello.

Children adore her.
My mother claims they are just attached
to her pink pelicans, bribe of cookies.
But I reckon it is more
something about her slowness
dangle of shawl, rhinestone hair clips
obsidian chimes
the way she clutches a wood cane
carved with the head of a sheep
leans on it to reach the back beds
where the pumpkins are waking
for the second Saturday in October
when we'll come over, pick one each
wheel it home in the barrow she's left out.

Venetian blind down
that's the way her parlor is come hot days
when the sun leaks no mercy
when she's seated on the porch
fiddling with her thread
or down in the shed gluing back

pieces of clay, colored glass
we find busted in the gravel.

My mother says she's an odd woman
but harmless of heart
macaroons will bribe any child
into becoming a fancy
that it's best I stay grounded in
my buffed penny loafers
catholic school uniform
faithful and faultless
if I am to take hold of life
step over every deft thing
not go vanishing.

PART THREE
The Color of Emptiness

A Coward, I Run Away from Your Picture Book Version of Paradise

You say our love crested
when I was still desirable
back then not now
two kids later
wrung out like some washcloth too many
hands have flogged across the floor.

It's not pleasant to be sized up
eased out like the way we shuffle
old people into retirement homes
boxcar children.

I will resurrect myself as a goddess I tell you
but you don't listen
expect me to take hold of life
with a firm grip
be a lean machine
acrobat of achievement.

Make way for Paradise
the sign will read
you and I vandalizing the bed
over and over
till nothing of you is left.
You did ask for fitness, didn't you?
The conquest of fragility has its price to pay.

It Was Such a Season

My yellow eyelid opens
morning over a serrated pillow.
The wallpaper taunts me
lauds a different life
meadows of peony
sheep grazing
willows.

You claim you can't see me
just my mulish equators
intention to tap terrestrial
out of the feeblest key.
You will leave nothing when you are gone
you proclaim, matter of fact
as if my volition fails
I am a blue asylum.

My yellow eyelid opens
morning over a serrated pillow.
The wallpaper rides in a pastel hearse
boasts Monet's gardens at Giverny
big headed peonies beside water

their pink flamed flirtation pinned wordless
onto the room's beige space
identical leaves forced to laud over
the window's conferencing.

Tell me –
where will you go
when my nails scratch
the emblem of death
in you?

Purgatory

August erodes my yellow sundress
invades plastic
cramped shoes.
I attach vagrancy to my hair
the way some people attach wings
slick handled words
perfumed egress.

If there is a purgatory it must
feel like this
the sun streaked water
before the fall
girls with barely any name
occupation, house
to call their own.

You dial vamp out of my
outworn premonitions
fishnet stockings, poems
as if I am more than a death wish
can sit in a room
sing to you
about the trials of nasturtium
majesty of bees
the man who boasts magic tricks
turns his blue heart shirtless

about girls who travel naked
mouth organ the moon
for a kiss.

Prayer

I crushed the eye of the preacher
who sees god riding a cannonball
through every sod field

pray for repentance
like some people pray for magic
conjure rabbits out of mohair.

Is it too late to inflate the world
imagine it succulent
unbustable?

You have a smooth tongue
slide words
make them artillery
shrill inventories of want
in a territorial landscape.

I cup my lips around the word *worship*
as if I can sidle the rain
turn a stock yard into meadow
as if my life depends on it.

Shoeless

So what if the pinwheels of happiness
bypass my gate
I am left shoeless
contemplating no moon
no lover with hands durable
enough to mine me.

Not everyone contemplates heaven
with equal remorse
finds the wild lupine.

It is Tuesday.
Some things remain unnavigable
desolate as the first day's calm
crushed open when sin entered.

I clear rocks from my throat
gather twigs
set kindling for the pyre
that will be my bed
infamy not by remorse
but by disposition.

Even a desiccated being
has the right to garner
her own flame.

Riddled with Bees

I thought it was corruptible
to live life like this
going through the motions
telling people only what
they wanted to hear
reserving paradise for the hereafter
because we slaughtered this one away

told you *I'll bust if I have to stay here*
navigating a pruned landscape
that hides its dismay.

You said I was cheeky
as in riddled with bees
car congestion
Queens quick talk.

Now I patrol cemeteries
raise the dead to elfin thrones
sprinkle holy water
over the hillsides of plastic roses
watch their wilted stems
grow prosthetic limbs
violet kisses.

The Man Who Imagined Me X-Rated in a Picture Gallery

It was scary to think I could go from
brown to platinum just by his gaze.
He had too many wants
couldn't hear the chinks
know I was a foreigner in chintz clothing
bought me black fishnet stockings
red enamel
suction cupped my body around midnight.

I told him -*you eat like a predator in my bed*
he brought his own meals after that.
I went from platinum to sepia
September an altar of crumpled leaves
the differential between loving and eternity
a coin lost in an orphaned shoe.

One morning my bed was covered
with dead fish
I knew it was time to go.

After the Timbre of Your Lovely Hands Go to Invent New Things

with this ring
with this ring
the promise of pampered feet
dabbled water
a blue hammock.

One day I find a river of blood
beneath the table
the formica refuses to come clean
frost leaks a ruined woman
carries away my lace
the colored lights I strung
with a summer hand.

The power fails
the house is invaded by moonlight
I pull my faux leopard muff
from the trunk
a marooned princess
wedded to snow.

You have gone now
how easy this vanishing.
Snow falls
I am august with ruined hope
all night find myself
rowing toward heaven with
an empty plate.

In the quiet rehearsal of my room
want to imagine only lovemaking.

The Color of Emptiness

I won't count on luck anymore
the way some children count marbles
cashiers count twice to make sure
of the correct change

will place my hands in a volcano
my body in an incinerator
see what that brings
no more herculean feats
contoured body
never able to lounge in its wanton.
I will enter decay
embrace the slow irreversible whittling
remember my mother
whose eyes lapsed from this world
long before her heart.

It will serve me right
to turn the table
enter neglect, claim it
sit on a park bench amid
pigeon poop, old people
wait for nothing to arrive
pronounce itself, rise up

girl who exiles the smugly esteemed period
declarative sentence
elopes with sin, dissolution
the color of emptiness
regressive clause
question mark that never
needs answering.

Magic Act

I wanted to disappear.
It was like a magic act
you disappear
might not come back
Alice through the looking glass
the camellias with their yellow tongues
blistering April
all the boys who thought they could
stickpin me to the wall
this life that kept bleeding me.

Jesus disappeared when the cross
couldn't hold him
when the rock from the tomb was
removed of its weight
disappeared but promised to come back.

But Eloise, my friend two doors down
won't come back
wore cotton socks planted with trees
shoes too small
got sidewalled by a truck
crossing the street one day.

My mother says children always reach heaven
faster than the rest
that's why I've vowed never to grow old
be like a rabbit shedding fur
white coat glistening
the coronation pink of my eyes
way magicians find rabbits
docile and soft

pliable enough to move through
obstructions, a hard table
come back.

Eloise thought the whole world
wore muddied galoshes, a dented pail.
I don't believe that.
It's blue as blue ices in a heat wave
blue as the arched pagodas
that marry the opposite lip of my cereal bowl.

Before Eloise went away
it was the disappearing part I wanted
in the cargo trunk of the basement
beneath the school desk.
I didn't know the terrible cost of erasure
under the forgotten shade tree
the anguish of the mute phone
voiceless bird calling
to live life invisible without the return.

Now I want the return
the miracle of the drowned child
brought back to life
the boy squatting six foot down
buried beneath an avalanche of sand
who converses with worms, crabs
the lost metal rings in his head
gets dug out, no longer afraid
how he cleaves to a different tune.

I want the wave of the magician's hand
the blue, blue song.

Snow

All night I talk to the
wind's wet tongue
the clothesline flapping
want in the side yard.

I am not sure I know how
to save things
gather the past
make a different kind of testimony
out of the world's stickpins.

Do shoes ever grow old with new tongues
one day will my fake leopard muff
appear unsodden with mildew
the white coat of winter
find me not wanting
for her ice palace in the snow?

Hope comes from
the early devouring of winter.
I apostrophe want
nail icons to my door

become the young girl skating circles
on the thick ice below the snow.

Toni Thomas lives in Portland, Oregon. Her poems have been published in Austria, Spain, New Zealand, Canada, England, Scotland, and Australia. In the United States her work has appeared in over fifty literary magazines including *Prairie Schooner, North Dakota Quarterly, Hayden's Ferry Review, the Minnesota Review, Notre Dame Review, Poetry East*, and more. She has been twice nominated for a Pushcart prize, and won several awards. She has published seventeen collections of poetry and four books for children.

Her figurative clay sculptures have been shown in gallery exhibits in Portland and Chicago, displayed in literary magazines, and housed in private collections in the U.S. and England.

Her short documentary *One of Us* was shown at the Trans-ideology: Nostalgia festival in Berlin and at the Museum of
Contemporary Art in Taipei.

Since Toni loves to create and sits buried in reams of poems, manuscripts, clay figures and images….she likes to imagine all of them out in the world
swaying wild as the lupine.

tonithomaspoetry.com

www.ingramcontent.com/pod-product-compliance
Lightning Source LLC
Chambersburg PA
CBHW021132080526
44587CB00012B/1247